Pumpkin Butterfly

Poems from the Other Side of Nature

Pumpkin Butterfly

Poems from the Other Side of Nature

Heidi Mordhorst

Illustrations by Jenny Reynish

WORDSONG

HONESDALE, PENNSYLVANIA

To Fiona, Daisy, and Duncan—
thanks to you, life is truly juicy!
—*H.M.*

To my family
—*J.R.*

Text copyright © 2009 by Heidi Mordhorst
Illustrations copyright © 2009 by Jenny Reynish
All rights reserved

Wordsong
An Imprint of Boyds Mills Press, Inc.
815 Church Street
Honesdale, Pennsylvania 18431
Printed in China

CIP data is available.

First edition
The text of this book is set in 13-point Minion.
The art is done in watercolor.

10 9 8 7 6 5 4 3 2 1

Contents

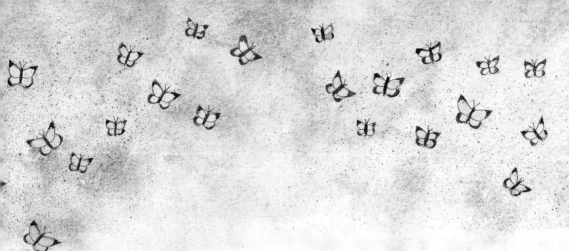

Ghosts

we haul our empty wagon to a patch of hilly earth
weighed down with heavy orange
burdened with cumbersome pumpkins

"This is the one"
"And this one"
we say

we cut the tough vines   and turn to load them up

behind our backs
a gust of butterflies rises and tumbles
on hot October air

yellow-green tinged with orange
wings as weightless and angular
as the pumpkins are heavy and round:

the ghosts of our pumpkins   untethered from earth

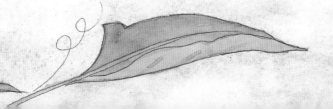

Plenty

"Just one show"
"Just two cookies"
     —that's all we're allowed,
       not enough!

"Too much glitter"
"Too much glue"
     —not enough,
       not nearly enough!

But here under the trees
are a trillion falling leaves
     mounding and drifting and tickling and piling
     curling and crumbling and blowing and flying
     drying and musting of summer's rusted heat

We dig in, bury ourselves—
leaves in abundance, plenty of leaves
     —enough,
       finally enough!

In Praise of Squirrels

just for being out
in broad daylight
in every yard and park

prudent nut hunters
fools flinging themselves
from tree to tree

high-wire acrobats
daring over busy roads
secret diggers in the dirt

harmless, fearless
minding their own bushy business
neither fierce nor tame

nobody's and everybody's
winsome wildlife pet
frisky whisky yes indeed

but praise be to squirrels
how willingly they share
their neighborhood with us

Cauldron Full of Compost

I'm raking for dollars when I find it—
    my red kindergarten lunch box,
    buried deep under leaves and tangled ivy
    between the playhouse and the herb garden.
I guess plastic really does last forever.

I fixed a lot of food in this lunch box:
    boiled summer cauldrons full of onion-grass spaghetti,
    mixed pans of mudluscious spring brownies,
    scooped great heaping mountains of snow cream
sprinkled with sugar, garnished with icicles.

And once, on Uncle Mark's birthday,
    I filled it with oozing mulberries
    and tiny wild strawberries
    tossed with encourage-mint.
Everyone ate that for real.

Who knows what I last cooked in here?
    Now nature's doing the brewing: a dark sludgy soup,
    a decomposing mess of dead plants laced with worms.
    A few of the leaves are new enough—
I can tell which are walnut, tulip, maple—

But most have moldered here so long
    they're part of the primeval stew.
    I stir it with a wooden spoon gone greenish
    with moss, drag up a dripping clump, spread it wetly
at the foot of the maple, richer and thicker than syrup.

With this dead soup I feed the tree.

Most Realistic Costume Award

Trick sneaks under the gate
black-sleek
queen of scratch   queen of screech

lying low
slipping   spilling   chasing treats

spine-stretch
crouch   creep

pounce!   she's got one
she's caught it like a bird
in her sugarsharp teeth
a little candy bird flapping
cellophane wings

Trick sneaks under the gate
blink-slink
howl-yowl   queen of prowl

far   near   disappear

Fireplace

It's only because of
the low December sun bearing
down along the street
that I notice
half a dozen fires without flame
smoldering among the roots of

a monumental oak where
leaves and fat acorns have pooled.
Their whispering columns of smoke
climb the trunk,
turning it into a risky thing:
a chimney made of wood.

I follow the white morning beams,
mingle my clouded breath with
the twisting wisps of smoke, and
warm my hands
over the burning of those
acorn coals, of that timber chimney.

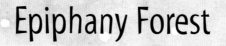

Epiphany Forest

On January 6th, when the presents
and carols and cookies are over,
there's one last thing to do.
Just as the Wise Men finally arrive,
we undecorate, unlight, strip away the gold star.

On the morning of the 7th,
at the bare, gray schoolyard
one by one our dying, drying trees,
still in their stands, are planted
among the cold poles of the equipment.

And on the 8th, when the
first snow finally arrives,
we fly out onto the playground
faster than the flakes are falling
to marvel at our frosted Epiphany Forest.

Winter Linens

Just water
solid water
just water frozen white

clinging to every leaf and chunk of gravel
lying along every twig and wire
mounding over every stump and silent ball

and in the dawning light
this water frozen white
glows cold and comfort both

as if to step out and lie down in it
to sink into the layer that lines the slope of the slide
would be a cozy coming home to bed.

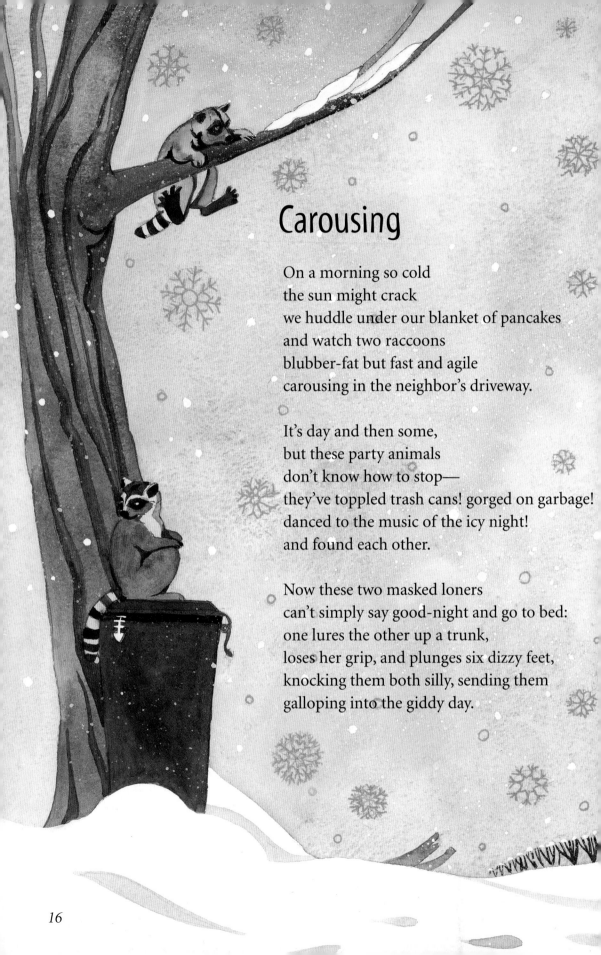

Carousing

On a morning so cold
the sun might crack
we huddle under our blanket of pancakes
and watch two raccoons
blubber-fat but fast and agile
carousing in the neighbor's driveway.

It's day and then some,
but these party animals
don't know how to stop—
they've toppled trash cans! gorged on garbage!
danced to the music of the icy night!
and found each other.

Now these two masked loners
can't simply say good-night and go to bed:
one lures the other up a trunk,
loses her grip, and plunges six dizzy feet,
knocking them both silly, sending them
galloping into the giddy day.

Frozen Angels

We line up and hold hands
knees locked
     then let go
Falling blindly, keen to feel
the crunch as we break the
     perfect snow

Arms drag and legs plow
high and open
     shut and low
Doing slowly jumping jacks
flat on our backs in
     heavy snow

We sit up and bend knees
balance out
     on booted toes
Stepping deeply, keen to see
the shapes we made in
     crumpled snow

There they are: our angels frozen
on their backs
     in a row
Where the cheerful field should lie
an angel graveyard
     in the snow.

The Horse in My Throat
for Duncan

Remember that raw day in February
when you told the aching truth?

"the horse in my throat
is a red dragon-horse
his roaring burns me up
in hot strawberry smoke

his hoofs and claws
are rough and sweet
my voice is tangled
in the beating of his wings

he's a thirsty horse
hungry for lemon and honey
but if I feed him
he'll whinny and fly away"

Petaling

People come crowding to these chilly streets
to see the twisted old cherry trees
crowded with new pink blossoms.

I come walking one week later.
Now the blossoms are breaking,
blowing, blizzarding petal by petal.

The wind lifts them, waves of petals the size
of my thumbnail, sends them rolling,
riding, racing on their ragged edges.

They're not *like* tiny, petal-soft wheels—
they really are tiny wheels of softest petal,
pedaling these streets toward summer.

Night Luck

Night is deep in a dark box
deep in a cushion of down
    nestled in tissue
    tied with ribbons
Night is asleep in the dark

Night wakes with curious paws
wakes in a furry fog
    wrestles the tissue
    nibbles the ribbons
Night is awake in the dark

Night tumbles in velvet directions
tumbles along to your bed
    sniffing your wishes
    wagging your worries
Night is a friend in the dark

Shell Game

everything
about an egg is
smooth or round or cool
the shell   pin-thin and brittle
the yolk   a little mound of sun
the white   sticky-thick and spreading

resting still as a stone in your palm
everything about an egg
is nothing like
a chick

April Gale

Oh, how the wind howls,
howls the blossoms from the boughs;

Oh, how the boughs bend,
bend and willow to the ground;

Oh, how the ground wells,
wells with blossoms blown to hills;

Oh, how the hills sound,
sound a whisper pink and loud.

Solar-Powered Sun Puppet

the dark side of me
glowers inside
drags at the tips of my toes

it feeds on clouds
on rainy skies
and only my shadow knows:

> how heavy
> the day is
> how low the horizon
> how sodden
> and sad
> I am

then sweet sun punches a hole in the clouds
sizzles and swims in my eyes
my shadow spills out through a hole in my sole
my darker side hung out to dry

> howbrilliantthedayis!
> howhighthebluesky!
> how sudden and mad I am!

I'm sunny-side up
I'm pumped full of light
my silhouette dances on walls

now I can see clearly:
my dark doppelgänger
freed by the sun's high call

> my demon cast out, my shadow of doubt
> is the shadow that proves that I am

Guest List:
Charles Darwin's Garden Party

balsam fir
spotted dolphin
pink verbena
garter snake

    fragrant white water lily
    grizzly sow
    Crater Lake

gnarled piñon
Painted Hills
tag alder
red-bat pup

    bee balm and bluebonnets
    mountain lion
    fungus cup

swallowtail
coneflower
Death Valley
prairie dog

    Virginia creeper
    Keyhole Arch
    black-browed albatross

Moose Creek
paperbark
columbine
tiger shark

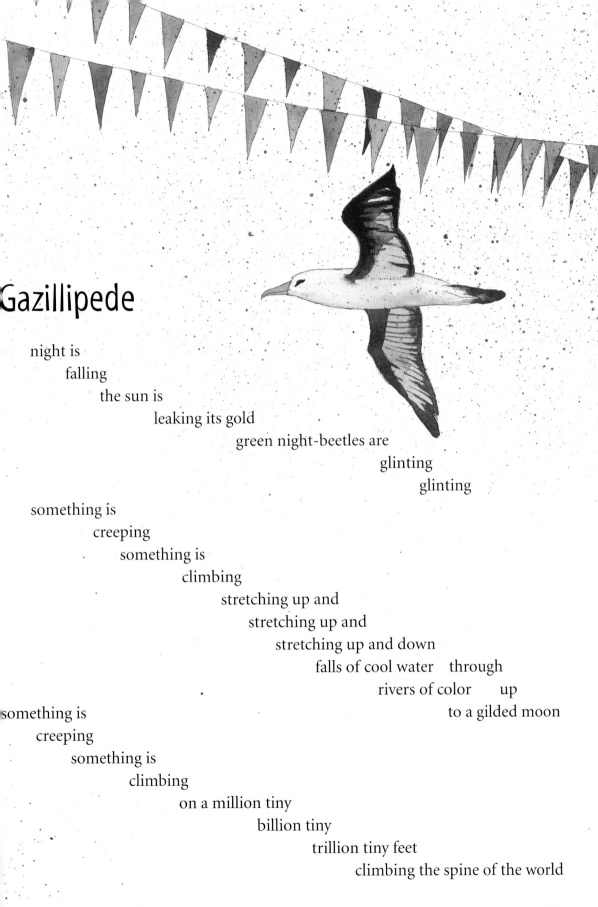

Gazillipede

night is
　falling
　　the sun is
　　　leaking its gold
　　　　green night-beetles are
　　　　　　glinting
　　　　　　　glinting

something is
　creeping
　　something is
　　　climbing
　　　　stretching up and
　　　　　stretching up and
　　　　　　stretching up and down
　　　　　　　falls of cool water　　through
　　　　　　　　rivers of color　　up
　　　　　　　　　to a gilded moon

something is
　creeping
　　something is
　　　climbing
　　　　on a million tiny
　　　　　billion tiny
　　　　　　trillion tiny feet
　　　　　　　climbing the spine of the world

Me Boy. You Plant.

After recess on Wednesday, red and sweaty,
I fall into my chair with the wobbly leg
and there you are, Plant,
in your raggedy pot—
my pal next to the teacher's desk.

Forgotten in the corner after Friday's fire drill,
you're as thirsty as I am, Plant,
your dusty leaves drooping just like
my bangs flop and stick to my forehead.

What we need, Plant, is a real fire,
just a small one—
the kind that would make
the ceiling sprinklers rain down
on your dry dirt, on my hot head.

Botanical Jazz

Quiet down, flower—
not so loud!

All this stretching your neck
and spreading your arms
bellowing your brassy yellow sass—

you're breaking our eyedrums
trumpeting all that color and sun
blowing that blazing yellow jazz. . . .

Belt it out, flower—
we'll join in!

Winged Solstice

At exactly the same stormy
watermelon moment

I clap one   the other strikes
into a jar flashing with fire   with a needle itching for blood

Cherry Very

Be sneaky, be cheeky
Pinch from the kitchen
The reddest, the roundest there are

A bowl full of cherries
A bowl of the very
Most cherriest bombs by far

Backbone straight
Step up to the plate
Puff up your chest and lungs

Swallow the fruit
Ready to shoot
Put the pit in the groove of your tongue

One more tip:
Round your lips
To launch it without a hitch

Don't get tense
Aim for the fence
Wind up like you're fixing to pitch

Now blast it hard
Across the yard
Kissing that missile good-bye

It's over the fence!
It's out of the park!
It's a letloose cherryjuice
    noschool slobberdrool
      spitwhistle summerfun home run!

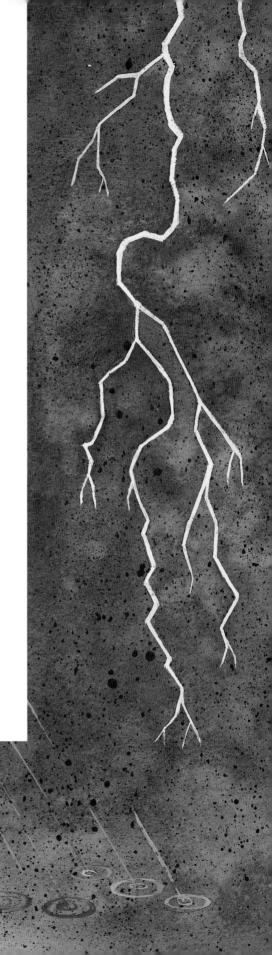

Something Dangerous

Nine o'clock midnight
storm pitching rain like
the first of forty days

Lie down in the street
in the middle of the street
in the middle of steaming June
streaming asphalt
shedding its day's heat

Halfway home
soaked right through
in a shirt full of holes

Lie down in the rain
lie down in the road
look up into the streaking sky
lie down
look up

Heaven might be
heaven might be this
dark and wet and dangerous